T0159004

Angel

Realm Builder

ANTONIO MIMS

authorHOUSE®

AuthorHouse™
1663 Liberty Drive
Bloomington, IN 47403
www.authorhouse.com
Phone: 1 (800) 839-8640

Published by AuthorHouse 09/27/2018

ISBN: 978-1-5462-5978-7 (sc)
ISBN: 978-1-5462-5977-0 (e)

Library of Congress Control Number: 2018910854

Print information available on the last page.

TABLE OF CONTENTS

CHAPTER ONE

Second Revelation

4,000 years after my soul never made it home again
this poem was born
six pounds of black fire
six ounces of hope
the screams are at their loudest
as nights chase me in and out of darkness
if ever these tears should find our eyes again
don't say we didn't warn you
the heat is forever
our last names will find you
brothers in too deep to fall back
two nights after the guns heard my sermon for the first time
asleep where victory explodes tears
the elders are dreaming pass last wishes
i found her first poem resurrected in a cloud ten breeze
fists filled with fire
an electric pulse
diving into stars
a new earth sees its first moments from the other side of
the sun
i kept writing
as if this land was a weapon and this trench was our heaven
searching for a marathon
this is what love made us
womb kisses
her magic is deadly
have you ever seen a heart shatter

and the shots are silenced by the screams
when skies split
dreaming of open days
revolving trances
and a torch
composing 30 names for each one her newborns
how many baptisms will our enemies run from before sunset
the smoke travels deep
her embrace is lethal
shooting flashbacks
back to back with destiny
i woke up trapped in a fight
who knew i'd live to see another page
following a freedom
faithful to its promise
the reward is priceless
paid in full
a life of hardships
too far in love to see defeat
too alive to die
where's my choke
she woke up screaming
shackled to broken promises
her savior has conquered another mountaintop
the rain is falling above vacant tombs
awaiting roaming souls as they exit the battlefield
i've heard machines argue against priests
as a congregation gathers down by a riverside
preparing for war
this world has been victimized by its own lies
i've seen governments fall to their knees

candidates crawling over courtyard ruins
still collecting taxes at the crossroads
their followers are blind
the next time GOD speaks
i'll fly away
there were bombs beneath my tears
winds quaking through my nights
starlit skies at war against haunted thrones
a four floor 16 room pulpit filled with ghosts
this is the revolution that raised me
my older brother is the only trust i know
all of my soulmates are angels
i stayed awake while three dreams nursed my heartbeat back
to reality
nine dollars worth of liquor and no worthy challenge
4,000 years worth of fallen leaves going up in flames
last dances left lonely
now a sunrise's only cure is my latest poem
this was armageddon
no sleep
and a choice between drugs and true love
moon struck visions
and a faithfulness cherished by the masses
another sunday dinner with no next of kin
early morning flights back from love
this prayer will echo until forever is now

CHAPTER TWO

Ghost World Dreamer

hell searches for a home
and the riots take shape beneath shots into the night
the sun's reflection roams
dodging sirens
the sounds echo and the stars are opened
a prayer sent to my first love
a new day
the same war
earth's core
hollow
where stars build seeds and eternal life finds protection
the laws are afraid of the hourglass
reflecting an ancient eruption
pain
power
and love
a heart with no name
a blank face
eyes mesmerized in a blacked out daze
watching out for brighter days as they open behind closed
eyelids
a shadow with no fear
unlock the truth
let her spirit guide you
through mysteries and wonders
where creation searches for redemption
souls beat rapid as skies collapse

inside hollow dreams
wisdom is the writer's last hope
mountains surrounded by possibilities
world leaders' greed and a coward's betrayal
as i stand face to face with this never-ending struggle
i can see the fear in his eyes
his soul is torn between right and wrong
heaven was rewritten by the wisdom in my palm
GOD is the only claim i own
where price tags and body bags share the top of a bottomless
food chain
not enough time to think
the writer only has one pledge
one second too late means you won't escape november's firing
line
seven spirits of death trapped in chases
a savior's war
frozen electric clashing chills
made in heaven
true peace and a salvation streaming
stinging in the darkness
if the riddle had gotten any longer
hell would still be a place
instead
their troops are still dying
as if these war games were just a myth and the murder rate
would never get this high
i remember the day the sky split with the weight of 2,000
easters on its back
a stay house at every planet's six

this is a flooded ball of fire
alive and manic inside a crazy dream
widows counting rose petals
the writer's hand
clutching one dozen stems
at sun's core
we create fire and send shots
our enemies are too afraid to approach us
how many more of her own lies can her soul take before it
explodes
if bombs had minds of their own would my poems still
enchant you
bending neon sunrays until the darkness retreats
winds with no dwellings
soaring
seeking children of the promise
protecting earth from destruction
the souls are screaming for justice
i'm rehearsing scriptures on a flooded park bench
the fire is everywhere now
when roses were rocks trapped in vapor
this is the color of heaven at river's end
where the waters fall
where stones receive new names
as an older earth bleeds gold from its core
a longing only her king can fulfill
soulmates reborn in a dual prism
her reflection is the only kiss i know
private planes circle us daily
the feds will never incarcerate my truth

i'm warring against colonizers who are determined to hunt
down heaven
protecting our homeland we stood against law enforcement
and we fought off officers of the court until our knuckles bled
us answers to our prayers

CHAPTER THREE

The Black Testament

Met with a prayer
a war cry echoes
piercing thru the pain
torn from a daughter's revenge
as the family prepares for another battle
heaven is silent
i watched an angel exchange its wings for a gun
alone on a broken street corner
stalking a day worth three dollars and a lifetime of trouble
stalking its own reflection
i never thought this angel would ever make it home again
face to face with a law enforcement choking on fear
this is frontline page one standards
when rules are broken
alive on halfdead streets
a church finds its fate beneath flames
the family is marching
our enemies don't know who to trust
face to face with a government hung from a noose made of
regrets
thinking back to when i cherished peace
i've gone far pass crazy
refusing to forgive or forget the torment and every attempt
to see me destroyed
where freedom is worth more than safety
GOD's army is eternal
winds trained by grace

a prophecy mapping missions to save daughters and raise
sons
free from oppression
stolen lands plotting revolts
a heavy heat armed with seven red stars
heartbeats explode
blinks stashing dreams inside tears
the angel has no choice but to gamble
flames and shadows
the sky trembles
no apologies
no retreat
where cops keep a gram of cocaine handy
i'm six days in
staring at my first felony conviction
this is round one
on the other side of a line this county will wish it never
crossed
the fight is forever
the arresting officer is lost in his own tyranny
GOD has made it back to his throne
as the angel escorts my soul back to earth
where will this war end
this is ghost world deep in thought
cloud ten is building new weapons
as hell leads this world into a bottomless pit
i'm one step away from victory
and the family is praying for its savior
we will create community with an intent to cultivate a newer
and more perfect love
violence and peace will have their place

the judgment will have its day
inside of a night where law enforcement is defeated
live free and never die
i am not a person
i am a people
we barge in with explosions beneath our wings
i brought my entire city with me
excuse us but may i please speak to your sergeant
this is our war on poverty
inside freedom
inside our liberties
we feel like magic
cloud ten forever
this is coming to america
the second installment
i am a part of a war displaced
a path towards reconstitution and reconstruction
political empowerment within poverty-stricken populations
colonization versus environmental justice
war fostered by service and protection
religion
royalty
and riches

CHAPTER FOUR

God House

Nights like these never end
behind eyelids made of flames
dreams racing from earth into the heavens
renaming stolen ambitions
the writer's touch is deadly whenever i see blood
as the smoke chokes her tears into submissions
i prepare for the next battle
up to my neck in prayers
too strong to let this feeling go
stepping far pass a last wish
sentenced to a plantation
cultivated atop years of violence
war was all that our dreams knew
this pulpit was our only way to escape the tyranny
at trance volume is an empty envelope
and a shepherd returned from the dead
a prophet eclipsed by red writing and no drop zone
creation's first tomb
a whisper held by promises
promises too powerful to be broken
how many saviors like us do you know
three lifetimes reborn inside the daydreams of a six-year-old
a slave revolt relived every night
it's four a.m. again
the march home is timeless
my wings are restless
reckless haste

manic shots
our shooter is champion
his fire is eternal
hell fears the rush
there's blood on the market
a cow's mouth on the flag
i let the powers separate in my sleep
the next morning it was payroll classics and boom time on
doom's day shore
a 30-building chase
i'm watching myself save the earth again for the third time
this month
i shoot first and never let the lies take my power
the laws are afraid of my gift
her dance is my only protection
this gun is the only answer
and i never let the bounties see me sleep
you'll never see me again
baptized in a dream
color every light ghost
and if you're caught
chew glacier at sun speed
i'll make the sky cry the hardest times ever
and i never give it a second thought
how massive the power of loyalty is
a dream that will never end
awake inside her embrace
demons lurking beneath heartbeats
the honeymoon is over
we're headed back to the motherland
the family is safe

marching with clinched fists
clutching eternities
every step is another battle
and if you're caught
ask GOD
i go in deep
my poetry is my magic
dark set at high tide
a killer's creed
a murder's host
i'm dream made and undefeated
my ghost is GOD
my blood is eternity's canvas
as the ashes come to life and take flight flying above
aftershocks
there's no way out
flooded skies
too angry to breathe
and when this conversation started it was just about money
but i count quick
embracing the foreverlasting and 17 different chokes
my mischief is prince of star born
your death is nothing but a good sale
some say i grind too hard
as if this book is all mine
i say nothing
writing from a red zone
backbone deep
for a twin and one cellmate
no repeat
let the silence love you

i close my eyes and the sermons recite themselves
dreams awaken
surrounded by fire
heaven's pain
skies baptized in love
wars printed beneath my eyelids
where the hits land the hardest
i woke up in an empty basement with blood on my hands
a cold sweat became a summer storm
she closed her eyes and watched me thug my way through
this dream deserves a title
the next night never ended
if ever there were a peace so great
protected by holiness
the vultures lurk
seeking to devour the innocent
our grace is pure and the lessons guide us into lifetimes that
connect our past with our future
past lifetimes awaken
trapped between hell and heaven
a savior's calling
protected by a warrior's wisdom
this is our prayer for redemption

CHAPTER FIVE

Cloud Ten Forever

there's a jezebel on every corner and the gun store never closes
my last fight hit to close to home
i can still see his ghost face down on the pavement
now i float between seasons
if ever there were a GOD he would be invisible
invincibly chill
in the corner of every room war ready with a loaded pistol
surrounded by eight million ghosts
eight million apostles who died then returned as epistles
if ever you need me
i'll be outside selling a hard ticket
i am silence in the flesh with three tears left that i cherish
like a best friend
how will we make it home
far from my final breath
trusting in a flame
resting on raging winds
dreams chasing my soul into never-ending poems
i can hear myself reciting blue notes over black skies
holding prayers for freedom in my palms
a hard-sung melody's echo
my mother's voice carries me away
when will eternity build a refuge for our tears
awaiting my final heartbreak
our GOD is fearless
his children are brave

dark set sent
never lost
inside wires
blaze blizzard touch
never caught
clutching her love letters
how many lies do you have left
how many times have you seen the sky shatter
i am ocean's twin
on every planet's edge
coast roam romantic
our enemies are addicted to sleep
resurrections are the wings of the spirit
as the blood is shed these poems provide healing
the churches are haunted and the crossroads haven't seen
daylight in40 days
reforming my mind from a maze to a battlefield
gathering weapons
this is the color of the race i run
waiting for death to show its face
their armies are drowning in a widow's tears
far from home
i am marching into her greatest fears
my brother will return accompanied by a consuming fire
he will lead us to our destiny
i can hear winds chasing justice
sky tomb electric
solar heaven trench
wild land surface
reflections of wars won
the dark drift

detonation on sight
sent from above the stars
beyond opaque nights
these are the survival methods that define my culture
the smoke ain't been this loud since my twin was trapped in
the city of angels cussing out cops
heaven is not hiding but it is hidden
a flame too dark
a father too heartless to sleep
eyes of the dead
this is where life starts
red winds
ghosts of the dreamer's heartbeats
at the edge of creation's foresight
before the war woke up
i'm still black spirit
seven red dots
golden axis
gold grid
new magic
trance shot
from the heart
i murdered your maker
timeless victory
eras anchored in weather systems
headed to heaven
we join hands
fire replaces our flesh
love made by an angel and her prince
our bodies vanish as spirits resurrect our heartbeats in a star's
reflection

drenched in holiness
surrounded by its essence
our enemies have fallen
death has met its match
it's kill season because i said so
shadows swarming
darker mornings
eclipsing exhausted prayers
i'm too brave to quit
let it rain
i'm in love with a goddess
crowds on every decimal
flammable contacts
death electric
timebombs and dollar signs
can you feel the heat
back from the future
he died choking on a microphone
as my enemies close in
i rep my trench
i woke up with blood on my hands
i will write you to death
who do you believe in
every dollar day is fixed
listening to my album for the eighth time today
headed to ghost world escorted by herb smoke
i'm cloud ten forever
for whoever wants to die next
it's the reaper
storming through realms
i will find you

all black tetris where the matrix has no exits
war written age old blueprints to an ocean
tattooed on every planets' edge are stars racing into the
reflection of an empress
eloping with moonlit power
this is still line one
life land
load heavy
explode
roaring
war ready
no more chances
another hard hit
made in fire
for forever
danger closing in
i am the bomb
longing for justice
my brother will be home soon
none better than the twins
replacements
paper thin saviors
sound off silence holders
i love my queen
hold me closer
this is real magic
it's always heaven when we write it
be ready
these are the wings of time
gasping for resurrected dreams
listening to the songstress

as her poems become miracles
and i murdered your GOD last night
the hard pack
on a line push
ransom on a sure shot
that's the business
war time
the mainstream
flying inside airwaves
the writer's greatest weapon
when love was a spirit
you can't silence the songstress
my soul will disappear
her ghost knows my secrets
the nightmares are racing against themselves
the city is at war for its savior
i'm headed back from the future
don't ever dare my prophecy
read my book twice then bury it under a stone in africa
it's a promise
i won't go back to heaven until all of my enemies are dead
and gone
dolphin in the sky
standing on hard-drop
lands promised
lesson learned
the movement
forever
never say die
or feel like life isn't worth the fight
walking into futures

feeling too high to hold the tears back

breaking into new beginnings

marching over oceans

swallowed by darker skies

silent nights

shooter reward

westward

toward the take

handguns and love made by ghetto music and orchestrated
    mischief

my mind is weapon

when heaven was my mother's only friend

and my smile was her only hope

electric sky

please tell me my future

electric sky

i'm going to choke you to death when i find you

CHAPTER SIX

Peace Keeper Planet

Nurtured within teardrops of revenge
cradled by bravery
an end zone ten neighborhoods deep
fueled by campfires and bloodshed in the faces of blind
horizons
protect the homeland
it is a 1,000 mile walk from here to ringside
130 pounds of hurt
marching with a prayer
one first -round -knockout later
i'm dragging the soul of his ghost up a coastline towards a
forest built by firestones
x-ray solar
flare laser frontline
plantation army battleplans
divine and militant
for freedom and a kiss goodnight that will last until sunrise
i'm too smart to be afraid or put under arrest
the peace is pure and undefiled
three flames saved his daughter from a lesson too hard to
swallow
i remember when she was only three years old
trapped in a nightmare
sent from a caged quake locked behind prison walls
lives riddled
war written
golden when the promises are kept

GOD magic
heavy in season
louder than my heart's first beat
the first time i seen a ghost was in the mirror
the next time you think we are not real gangsters check the
body counts
war without terms
black klan
no give backs
we don't give up
you're at war against the king
streets missing from bitter days
a kiss for every time she whispers my name
the story ends every time
so now we color everything with maroon masonry
sunsets built by lawless winds and my twin's book of poetry
the evil has found its fate
this world has found her price
the only thing safe about my baptism is its ruins
the only rock worth anything to me is buried under a burnt
down church
the first time i found GOD he killed me
the second time we seen each other he blessed me with a
bride
she is my soulmate
we construct dreams of eternal life
and fight anyone who acts too tough to be sent to hell
she is champion
i'm just waiting for the next time we get a moment to rest
awaiting our next mission
bedtime remedies haunted by true stories

chain-smoker escape routes
overtime and death dealers with no reflections
black boy refuge
a downtown comprised of green voices and one treehouse
wrecked slaveship planks one with the weather
this ocean is in love with a savior
my soulmates are rain maker's guardian angels
in hopes love and peace we fight the good fight of faith

CHAPTER SEVEN

Weather World Wars

nano monsoon classics
network symphony
nuclei spirits aligned and united
defending this gospel
a picture-perfect prophecy
dream made and delegated to destroy hell and defeat the
devil's armies
we are too many fires to compete against
walls standing on my head
a leader's last words
we are still mister man-child
as black as nothing you've ever seen
at land's lift
creation's fire
earning moments back from time
my last blink just buried another eclipse
from a future's promise to the next bomb
meet the pressure
engraved in justice
another open soul
years of silence
one night wedded
eloping eyelids with quivers
kill season hard time
scriptures marching back from darkness
a daughter's first words
dead glares warring against her laughter

a funeral and no dream to protect its ghost
classrooms filled with threats
the reaper's fate
in a city built by prayers
attack mode
i'm dedicated
17 paces away from the flames
17 heartbeats away from a new day
quaking glows
ghost world
tears heavier than pain
gun smoke
black lighters
another war won
17 blinks away from the sun
17 screams away from the cure
i pray my glares don't follow me home
the riot is forever
heaven is fighting for its queen
dual-spirits
air born
raised to defend this gospel
17 verses away from the rush
17 kisses away from the end of time
i'll never forget the day the trees felt me for the first time
this is 33 years aimed at wind-letters
sound sought stones pointed at impact
wind-finder-heat
vapor sonic torch
carried into my heart by victory
this is 33 years of my wit

the dark side of my thankyous'
if only black were just a skin color
would this race i run every night be the same thing as heaven
have you caught me yet
are the glaciers ready to join my army
this dream floats
ghost-twin-spirit
smokes
liquor
and slave revolt planning
an island oppress proof
star body
dweller sets
a full house
no fallback
this is 33 years
and if i'm caught
bind these words within my heart
until the earth is reborn
release my soul from this chamber
my bones will become seeds
my mother's tears will never make it here again
your brother has been murdered
the laws fear the aftermath
anchored in anarchy
broken truces
prepared in patience
celestial armor
my one-man army
at war against your government
your

brother
has
been
murdered
your maker is next
i'm too young to be silenced
my poems are untamed reflections
searching for my voice
i'm never tired
my war atlas
i work hard to earn moments from time
the storm protects my sanity
death wishes and blind faith
three lifetimes worth a training
complete the mission at any cost
hustle hard and never fall
her love will find me again
her prayers are my only comfort
and if i'm caught
meet me at the end of this page
3,000 years later
the smoke will resurrect my truth
and the shots will remain
air born
airborne
brick walls falling into an empty sky
slick streets collapsing beneath eyelids
bleeding from the core
the next day i woke up frozen in a teardrop
30-dozen-roses
hot summer love

fights that have no name
family magic
one bomb away from victory
one step away from a kiss that will last forever
i sit in silence
awaiting her next wish
streets pacing through my veins
heat hovered
surrounding my soul
black ghosts baptizing roaming souls at the clock pool
this is one blink
shots sent into the night sky
from a plantation buried beneath a prison
a battleground afraid of itself
but i can still hear my angels' whispers
carried by screams
this is one blink
the laughter hurts when the tears have no one to choke
and the truth is marching through your veins like loud
thunder clapping at its enemies
her heart is pounding
who will she run to
i'm too focused to back down
wondering if this story has an ending
who's next to die
i'll be here
rehearsing blank pages
awaiting my next mission

CHAPTER EIGHT

Star Born

*a*s torches align
from the pulpit to your back porch
a street trenched by grace
one army
one face
a broken melody
chants as loud as skies split
a killer with no home
and sleep is death where i'm from
a fist raised above the stars
black klan
black power halo
four beasts lurking
police cars chased by firebombs
i'm too drunk and reloading too quick to exhale
calm and collected
prayers seeping from my pores
arrayed in frozen thunder
with a harder pulse
battling against fighter jets
i made love to an angel last night
this is midnight-sunlit-pastures
no callbacks
a life of hardships
LORD give me strength
conducting slave revolts every night
fire's departing

its longest colony
linemen deploy
GOD's mission
seeking the master's dead shift
cease trancing
blind's blizzard
eye hold
choking on wrath
one with the touch
and justice is a refuse to breathe
to live with the hurt
the hardest in
and if in axe
asking for blood
i remember nothing but her
tied in dual sun
twin moon
trench deep
GOD matrix
clutching mass suns
as roses forced power
lander war
in water
response
fisher net
explore
me and whoever else is ready
you
and
whoever else wants to die
this is guerrero

this is kato
all black pro-tecks
unified form
standard verse
peace keep with a kill-switch
mustard sip
saturn's soaker
summer mornings
hung-eloped
elite sight
see us thug
see me inside open fire
at worlds' endings
warring over seeds
danger screams
searching for sleep
death's hunt
seeking bodies
darker behind closed doors
no safety
just the reaper
and a few halfdead demons
screams suffocating prayers
screams pulsating thru the pain
the screams are alive
i won't rest until the nights turn to silence
one year
1,000 prayers
love's revenge
as the graves are opened
the static penetrates the sky

star-line-trace

searching for a peace to calm the masses from government
discord

while the wars hunt for another brown face

therefore we fight

to keep our forevers in secret

her best kept wish

red-fire-forever

and this is for those who have lied on love

you are at war against GOD now

The End

Printed in the United States
By Bookmasters